4|9|12

SUSTAINING OUR NATURAL RESOURCES

Louisburg Library
Bringing People and Information Together

Jen Green

Chicago, Illinois

www.heinemannraintree.com

Visit our website to find out more information about Heinemann-Raintree books.

To order:

☎ Phone 888-454-2279

💻 Visit www.heinemannraintree.com to browse our catalog and order online.

© 2012 Raintree
an imprint of Capstone Global Library, LLC
Chicago, Illinois

Visit our website at www.heinemannraintree.com

Edited by Andrew Farrow and Adrian Vigliano
Designed by Victoria Allen
Original illustrations © Capstone Global Library Ltd.
Illustrated by Tower Designs UK Limited
Picture research by Mica Brancic
Production by Eirian Griffiths
Originated by Capstone Global Library Ltd.
Printed and bound in the United States of America by Corporate Graphics in North Mankato, Minnesota.

15 14 13 12 11
10 9 8 7 6 5 4 3 2 1

Library of Congress Cataloging-in-Publication Data
Cataloging-in-Publication data is on file at the Library of Congress.

ISBNs:
978-1-4109-4321-7 (HC)
978-1-4109-4328-6 (PB)

Acknowledgments
The author and publishers are grateful to the following for permission to reproduce copyright material: Alamy p. 37 © Inga Spence, p. 38 © Jim West, p. 39 © AGStockUSA; Corbis p. 4 © Greg Smith, p. 7 © Frédéric Soltan, p. 8 © Gerhard Egger, p. 11 © Gerald French, p. 15 © Paul Souders, p. 21 © Tom Bean, p. 22 © Gerd Ludwig, p. 24 Science Faction/ © Karen Kasmauski, p. 26 Reuters/© Tomas Bravo, p. 27 © Andrew Holbrooke, p. 28 Rubberball/© Mike Kemp, p. 30 JAI/© Nigel Pavitt, p. 31 © Karen Kasmauski, p. 35 Reuters/ © Nicky Loh, p. 41 © Juice Images; Getty Images p. 12 Iconica/ Frans Lemmens, p. 14 National Geographic/Michael Nichols; p. 17 Robert Nickelsberg, p. 18 AFP Photo/Khaled Desouki, p. 19 Mike Goldwater, p. 23 National Geographic/Tim Laman, p. 25 Stockbyte, p. 29 Bloomberg/Adeel Halim, p. 32 AFP Photo/Elmer Martinez, p. 33 Bloomberg/Mike Mergen, p. 40 AFP Photo/Boris Horvat; Photolibrary p. 36 Animals Animals/Glenn Vanstrum; Reuters p. 34 Shannon Stapleton; Shutterstock p. 5 © Eugene Suslo, p. 10 © Gary Whitton, p. 13 © Jim Parkin.

Cover photograph of woman's hands planting a seedling in Hebei, China, is reproduced with the permission of Corbis/ © Yi Lu.

We would like to thank Michael D. Mastrandrea, Ph.D., for his invaluable help in the preparation of this book.

Contents

Natural Resources and Sustainability...4

Nonliving Resources..10

Environmental Resources 14

Living World 20

Population and Resources..28

Sustainable Living..34

Facts and Figures..42

Glossary..*44*

Find Out More...*46*

Index...*48*

Words appearing in the text in bold, **like this**, are explained in the glossary.

Natural Resources and Sustainability

All living things need **natural resources** to survive. Natural resources are useful materials found in nature, such as water. They have supported life on Earth for over 3.5 billion years.

Using up nonrenewable resources

Many important natural resources are **nonrenewable**. This means they will eventually get used up. **Fossil fuels** such as coal and oil are at risk of being used up. These **fuels** power many things, from our cars to the heat in our homes. But our supplies of fossil fuels will run out one day. The burning of these fuels also damages the **environment** (our natural surroundings).

Cutting down forests

Wood from forests is an important natural resource. It is used as a fuel and as a building material. Forests are also cleared for farming or to raise cattle. These forests are **renewable**. They can be naturally replaced. New trees can be planted.

Once coal supplies run out, they run out forever.

But it takes hundreds of years for new trees to grow into large forests. Cutting down forests also damages the environment.

Damaging our environmental resources

Air, water, and soil support living things. Similarly, plants, animals, and other living things are food sources in nature. These all seem like resources that should always be renewable.

But human activity has placed many of these resources in danger. **Pollution** (harmful waste) is making the air, water, and soil unsafe. It is killing off many kinds of living things. Humans build and expand into new areas. As a result, the plants and animals that once lived there are harmed. Sometimes they are killed off forever.

Clearly, we are overusing Earth's natural resources. We are also hurting the environment in the process. So, how can we find a path forward?

These devices use a limitless, renewable resource: the wind. This could help us stop using nonrenewable resources (see page 13).

(see page 13).

WORD BANK

fossil fuel   fuel, such as coal or oil, that is made of the remains of plants or animals that lived millions of years ago

natural resource   useful material found in nature, such as water or oil

nonrenewable   describes resources, such as coal or oil, that will get used up

renewable   describes a resource, such as the wind, that will not get used up

Rising population

In the last 150 years, the human **population** (number of people) has grown rapidly. In 1900 there were 1.6 billion people on Earth. About 7 billion people are expected by 2011. Every year there are more mouths to feed. More **fossil fuels**, wood, and other **natural resources** are needed to make all the things we want or need. How can we meet this challenge?

What is sustainability?

"Sustainability" means using Earth's natural resources in a planned and careful way. This approach will meet our current needs. It will also save resources for the future. This way, resources will not get completely used up.

World population growth

Year	Population
1750	700,000,000
1804	1,000,000,000
1850	1,200,000,000
1900	1,600,000,000
1927	2,000,000,000
1950	2,550,000,000
1955	2,800,000,000
1960	3,000,000,000
1965	3,300,000,000
1970	3,700,000,000
1975	4,000,000,000
1980	4,500,000,000
1985	4,850,000,000
1990	5,300,000,000
1995	5,700,000,000
1999	6,000,000,000
2006	6,500,000,000
2009	6,800,000,000
2011	7,000,000,000
2025	8,000,000,000
2050	9,200,000,000

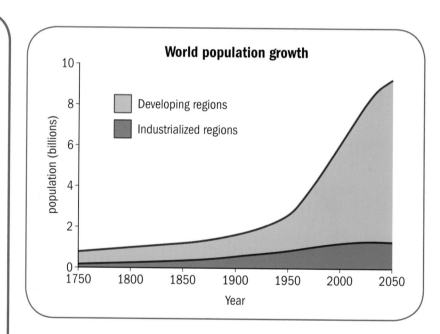

The chart (left) and graph (above) show the rise in human population from 1750 to 2050. Green shows poorer countries. Blue shows wealthier countries.

Sustainable development

The idea of sustainability began in the 1980s. Before that, people thought Earth's resources would last forever. Then, scientists realized that resources like oil, coal, and forests would one day run out. So, they came up with the idea of **sustainable development**. This means allowing people and businesses to move forward and develop—while saving resources for the future.

This family lives in a poor area of the city of Mumbai, in India. As the world population increases, it becomes a challenge to provide enough resources for everybody.

WORD BANK
population   number of people in an area
sustainability   using Earth's resources in a planned and careful way
sustainable development   managing economic growth and the way we live, without destroying resources that will be needed for the future

7

Ecological footprint

Something called an "**ecological footprint**" is used to measure the use of **natural resources**. In 2008 experts said the world's ecological footprint was 1.4 Earths. That means that people were using Earth's resources 1.4 times faster than they could naturally be replaced.

Sharing Earth's resources

But all countries are not using Earth's resources equally. Wealthy countries like the United States are known as **developed countries**. People in these countries use huge amounts of resources, such as food and oil. At the same time, people in poorer places, like Africa and South America, use 30 to 40 times fewer resources. Countries in these parts of the world are known as **developing countries**.

In developed countries, people need to use fewer resources. People in developing countries need to get a fairer share. This book will explore ways to achieve these goals.

This book will also explore humans' use and abuse of Earth's resources. As you read, take the **environment** challenge. Think closely about all sides of the issues. Then, decide on the best way forward. How can we learn to not use up all of Earth's valuable resources?

In developed countries, people use more than their fair share of Earth's resources. They also create huge amounts of waste.

Ecological Debt Day

Ecological Debt Day shows how quickly Earth's resources are being used up. The debt day is the date on which we use up all the resources that were available for that year. Once we hit this point, we start using up Earth's reserves (stored supplies) of resources.

Before 1986 our total use of the planet's resources was balanced by Earth's ability to create new resources. But in 1987 we used up our year's supply of resources by December 19. In 2000 the date was November 1. Every year, the date moves a little closer to the start of the year. Find out more at the Global Footprint Network, at www.footprintnetwork.org/en/index.php/GFN/page/earth_overshoot_day/.

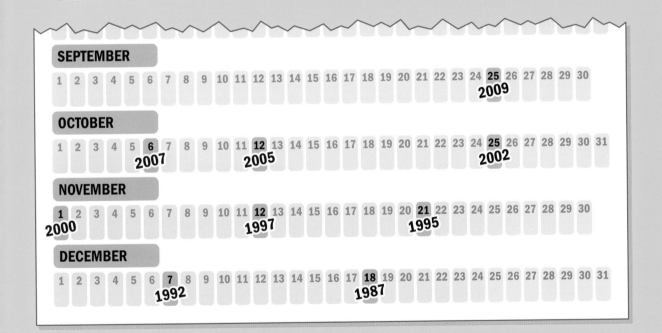

SEPTEMBER

1 2 3 4 5 6 7 8 9 10 11 12 13 14 15 16 17 18 19 20 21 22 23 24 **25** 26 27 28 29 30
2009

OCTOBER

1 2 3 4 5 **6** 7 8 9 10 11 **12** 13 14 15 16 17 18 19 20 21 22 23 24 **25** 26 27 28 29 30 31
2007 **2005** **2002**

NOVEMBER

1 2 3 4 5 6 7 8 9 10 11 **12** 13 14 15 16 17 18 19 20 **21** 22 23 24 25 26 27 28 29 30
2000 **1997** **1995**

DECEMBER

1 2 3 4 5 6 **7** 8 9 10 11 12 13 14 15 16 17 **18** 19 20 21 22 23 24 25 26 27 28 29 30 31
1992 **1987**

WORD BANK
developed country   wealthy country where many people live comfortably
developing country   country where many people do not live comfortably
ecological footprint   measure of human demands on Earth's resources
environment   natural world surrounding us on Earth

Nonliving Resources

Nonliving **natural resources** include things like rocks and coal. Getting and using these resources can have serious effects on the **environment**.

Mining

Mining involves removing valuable materials from the ground or below the surface. This process provides us with useful materials, including:

- **fossil fuels** (see page 12)

- **minerals** (hard, natural substances such as gypsum, which is used to make plaster and cement)

- **ores** (minerals that contain useful metals, such as copper)

- gemstones (such as rubies)

- rock used in construction.

These substances usually form very slowly. So, they are **nonrenewable**.

Effects of mining

Mining often has a lasting effect on the environment. Surface mining involves stripping away the covering plant life, soil, and rock. Deep-level mining involves building passageways and tunnels underground.

The Bingham Canyon Mine is in the state of Utah. It is the world's deepest open-pit mine. This photo shows how it has torn up local land.

Mining creates huge amounts of waste rock, known as **tailings**. Sometimes tailings are dumped into old work sites that have become empty pits. These pits often fill with water, forming lakes.

Minerals such as copper produce highly poisonous waste. This can leak into the soil. These poisons can also end up in lakes filled with liquid tailings.

CASE STUDY

Mining disaster in the Philippines

In 1996 there was an accident at a copper mine in the country of the Philippines, in Southeast Asia. The Marcopper Mining Corporation dumped tailings in a lake. The lake had formed from an abandoned pit. But the lake's system of drains failed. This caused lots of tailings to spill into local rivers. It killed all wildlife. A flood of poisonous waste spread to nearby farmland. This made crops unsafe to eat.

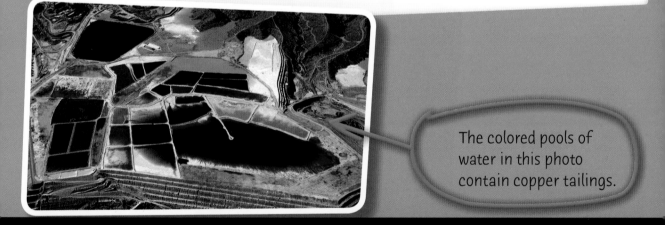

The colored pools of water in this photo contain copper tailings.

WORD BANK

mineral   hard, natural substance. Minerals help to provide everything from cement to gold.

mining   removing valuable materials from the ground or deep below the surface

ore   mineral that contains a useful metal, such as copper

tailings   waste rock left over from mining

Fuels

Fuels provide **energy**, or the ability to do work. This energy is used to power homes, factories, transportation, and more.

Fossil fuels include coal, oil, and **natural gas**. (Natural gas is a fuel **gas** found underground. A gas is a substance with no definite shape, like air.) Fossil fuels supply three-quarters of our energy needs. They formed from the remains of plants and animals. This process took millions of years. So, fossil fuels are **nonrenewable**.

Supplies of fossil fuels are already running low. So, oil companies must drill in far-off locations to find oil. In 2010, drilling in the Gulf of Mexico caused a huge oil spill. This will harm the local **environment** for many years. Burning fossil fuels also releases harmful air **pollution**. So, how else can we get energy?

The nuclear option

Nuclear energy involves working with a metal called uranium. This process does not release the same air pollution as fossil fuels. But, after it is used, uranium gives off harmful **rays** (lines or beams) of energy. Its waste cannot be disposed of safely. There is also the risk of deadly accidents.

Wood is one of the main sources of energy in **developing countries**. But to get it, trees must be cut down.

This factory in South Dakota makes a "**biofuel**" called ethanol. Biofuels are made from plant material. They are considered renewable, because new crops can be grown.

Renewable energy sources

The Sun, wind, and waves are other energy sources. They are **renewable**. Using them causes little damage to the environment.

Scientists are coming up with improved ways to use these and similar resources. For example, panels placed on roofs can use the natural power of the Sun. Or systems using windmills can turn the natural energy of the wind into power we can all use. Scientists hope to improve these systems and make them more widely used. This could create **sustainable** energy sources for everyone.

WORD BANK

energy   ability to do work
nuclear energy   energy made by using uranium
pollution   when the natural world is harmed by waste or other substances
sustainable   when resources are managed so that they do not run out in the

Environmental Resources

Living things need Earth's air, water, and soil. But human activities are harming these important **natural resources**.

Earth's atmosphere

The **atmosphere** is a layer of **gases** surrounding Earth. It protects us from harmful **rays** from the Sun. Certain gases in the atmosphere trap some of the Sun's heat. This causes temperatures on Earth to rise. This is called the **greenhouse effect**. We need temperatures to rise like this to have a planet that is suitable for life.

Changing climate

But in the last 200 years, we have added more **carbon dioxide** gas to the atmosphere. This is because carbon dioxide is released when **fossil fuels** are burned—for example, as gasoline in cars. Carbon dioxide is also released when forests are burned to clear land for farming. This release of gases is increasing the natural greenhouse effect. It is causing a dangerous rise in temperatures known as **global warming**.

People burn rain forests to clear land for raising animals. This adds to the carbon dioxide in the atmosphere.

Effects of global warming and climate change

Due to global warming, the last 30 years have had some of the warmest temperatures on record. Ice caps have started to melt. The melted water goes into oceans, raising sea levels. These changes caused by global warming are called **climate change**.

Scientists think global warming will make weather patterns change more over time. This could include floods, hurricanes, and long periods with no rain.

To reduce climate change, we need to stop using so many fossil fuels. We need to turn to **renewable energy** sources instead, such as Sun and wind power. In wealthier parts of the world, we also need to use less energy (see pages 40 and 41).

The world's ice is melting. The melted water adds to the amount of ocean water.

WORD BANK

atmosphere   layer of gases that surrounds Earth
climate change   change in the regular weather patterns of a region
global warming   rising temperatures worldwide. This is caused by an increase in gases in the atmosphere that trap the Sun's heat.
greenhouse effect   warming effect caused by certain gases in the air. They

Earth's freshwater

Living things need freshwater. Around 97 percent of all the water on Earth is salty. So, just 3 percent of Earth's water is freshwater. Of this 3 percent, over two-thirds is locked up as ice. Nearly one-third is located in underground layers of rock called **aquifers**.

This leaves just 0.5 percent in freshwater sources such as rivers, lakes, and swamps. But about 70 percent of this freshwater is used for farming. Look at the graph below to see just how much water is needed for different crops.

Wasting water

In **developed countries**, people waste a lot of water. Scientists say everyone needs about 50 liters (13 gallons) of water a day. In the United States, people use around 500 liters (132 gallons) a day. A lot of water gets wasted through leaking pipes, dripping faucets, and people taking long showers.

At this rate, people are using water faster than nature can make it. Because too much water is being used, rivers, lakes, and aquifers are running dry.

Huge amounts of water are needed to grow crops and raise animals for food.

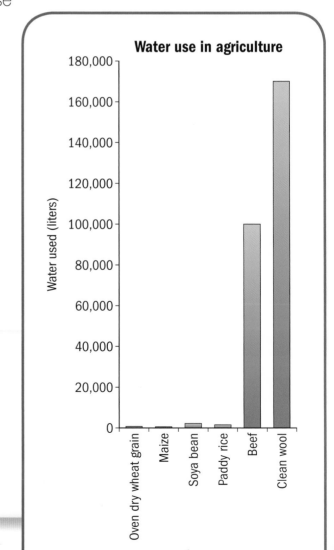

Water use in agriculture

Pollution and growing pressure

Pollution from wastewater, farming, and factories dirties many freshwater sources. In 2009, 2.6 billion people worldwide lacked enough **sanitation** (wastewater removal). Nearly 1 billion people are without clean water. This can lead to deadly health problems.

People can get sick from drinking water that is also used for bathing or washing.

CASE STUDY

Shrinking Aral Sea

The Aral Sea in western Asia was once the world's fourth-largest lake. But starting in the 1960s, large-scale **irrigation** projects changed this. Irrigation projects control the flow of water by using channels (paths for water to flow through) and other devices. These projects used huge amounts of water from the rivers that flow into the lake. As a result, the lake has lost about 90 percent of its water. Local fishing areas have been destroyed.

WORD BANK

aquifer   layer of rock or earth underground that holds water

irrigation   method of controlling the flow of water through channels and other devices

sanitation   removal of wastewater

Soil

Soil is a **natural resource**. It supports plants. Plants provide food for wildlife and humans. Soil takes many years to form.

Modern farming practices can harm the soil and the **environment**. In **developed countries**, most farmers use substances called **fertilizers** to grow more crops. When the fertilizers drain into local streams and rivers, they harm the living things there.

Many farmers also use substances called **pesticides** to control weeds and insects. But these pesticides also kill worms and other tiny living things that keep the soil healthy.

Loss of soil

Only about one-quarter of the world's land is good for farming. So, in dry parts of Africa, farmers often **graze** (feed) **livestock** such as cows on land bordering deserts. The animals strip the plant life there faster than it can be replaced. This makes the land produce no life.

As the world **population** grows, the need for food increases. In response, farmers cut down forests and plow up grasslands. This creates more fields and pastureland to grow food. But it also means cutting down trees and plants with deep roots. When the ground is stripped bare, it can quickly lead to **erosion**. The soil is worn away by the action of the wind, water, or ice.

In places such as Egypt, human actions have made the soil unusable for farming.

Make a KWL chart

Using books or the Internet, find out more about the effect of farming on the soil. A KWL chart can help you organize your research. "K" stands for "What I **k**now." "W" stands for "What I **w**ant to know." "L" stands for "What I **l**earned." Your main question goes in column 2. Fill in column 1 using the facts given here. New facts from your research go in column 3.

What I know	What I want to know	What I learned
Modern farming can damage the soil.	How does **pollution** affect living things in the soil?	

CASE STUDY

Expanding Sahara

The Sahel is a region south of the Sahara Desert, in Africa. It has very little rainfall. In the 1950s, people moved into this area. They began grazing livestock on the few plants there. They also burned woodlands to create areas for crops. Years without rain turned the unprotected soil to dust. The dust blew away on the wind. As a result, the Sahara Desert has expanded 40 kilometers (25 miles) south. But in parts of the Sahel, replanting is helping to restore the land.

The Sahel has suffered from lack of rain. Some experts link this to **global warming**.

WORD BANK

erosion   when rock or soil is worn away by the action of the wind, running water, or ice

fertilizer   substance that farmers use to make plants grow better

graze   feed on growing plants such as grass

pesticide   substance that farmers use to control weeds and pests

Living World

Many plants and animals provide people with food, medicines, and materials for things like clothing. But if we overuse these **natural resources**, there is a danger. We threaten Earth's **biodiversity**, meaning its variety of life.

Habitat loss

A **habitat** is a place, such as a woodland, that supports certain types of wildlife. Certain **species** (specific groups of living things) live in a habitat.

As the number of people rises, people need more land to grow food. They also need more spaces to live and work. Habitats such as wild grasslands are turned to farmland. Marshes (low, wet areas of land) are drained to build new roads, towns, and airports. Wild stretches of coast (land alongside oceans) become vacation resorts.

In nature, species **evolve**, or change, in response to changes in their habitat. This process happens gradually. But as humans bring rapid change to habitats, some living things cannot keep up. Some species do not survive major changes to—or the loss of—their habitats.

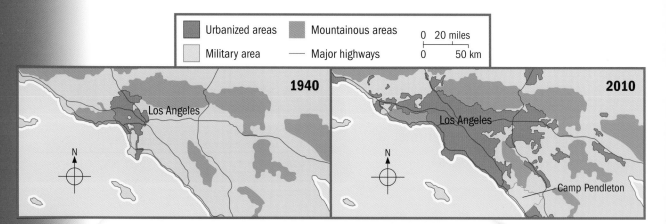

These maps show how the city of Los Angeles, California, has expanded over time. This kind of growth can destroy habitats.

Lost prairie

Before the 1800s, the Great Plains of the United States were covered with millions of acres of **prairies**. Prairies are largely treeless areas of grassland. These prairies were natural habitats for many kinds of plants and wildlife, especially prairie birds. But starting in the mid-1800s, Americans were spreading westward. They searched for areas to settle and grow crops. As a result, much of this wild habitat was plowed up and lost.

Today, groups like the American Prairie Foundation are working to bring back some of these lost habitats. You can read more about their efforts at www.americanprairie.org.

The once-wild grasslands of the prairies have been plowed up to grow crops.

WORD BANK

biodiversity	variety of life in a particular area
evolve	change over time to suit particular surroundings
habitat	particular place that supports certain types of wildlife
species	specific group of living things

Clearing forests

Forests cover around 30 percent of Earth's land. Rain forests have great **biodiversity**. They support many plants and animals. Local people have lived in the world's forests for thousands of years.

Forests are an important source for wood, plants, animals, medicines, and **minerals**. Forests are also important to the health of the whole planet. This is because they take in **carbon dioxide**. As we have seen (see page 14), carbon dioxide is a major cause of **global warming**.

Deforestation

About 45 percent of the world's rain forests have been cut down since 1850. Forests are cut down for their valuable hardwood. Forestland is also cleared to make way for roads, towns, farms, and more. Around 116,000 square kilometers (44,800 square miles) of rain forest are cut down each year. That is about the size of 2,400 soccer fields every hour.

Deforestation (the clearing of forestland) is putting thousands of types of plants and animals at risk. If current rates continue, there would be little forest left by 2100.

Since about 1970, the Amazon rain forest has been cut down at alarming rates.

Deforestation in Malaysia

Deforestation is happening faster in the country of Malaysia, in Southeast Asia, than in any other rain forest area. The Malaysian government has come under pressure to stop cutting down trees. People worry that this is adding to global warming. Malaysia responds that it needs the money from trees to develop its businesses and provide better lives for its people.

Animals such as the orangutan are in danger because of deforestation in Malaysia.

Why are forests valuable?

People value forests for different reasons:

- To local people, forests have been their families' homes for many years.
- To logging, **mining**, and other companies, forests are a source of money.
- To governments, forests provide valuable things to **export** (sell to other countries).
- To people concerned about the **environment**, forests keep the planet healthy.

Which viewpoint is closest to your own?

Fishing

In the 1900s, modern fishing developed rapidly. Today, deep-sea boats sweep their huge nets along the bottom of the sea. They capture tons of fish at a time. Fishing supports many people worldwide.

Overfishing

Over 90 million tonnes (100 million tons) of fish are caught worldwide each year. These levels are not **sustainable**. If they continue, the seas will be fished out. **Overfishing** occurs when so many fish are taken that not enough fish are left to have young. Some experts believe that 75 percent of the world's fish supplies are either fully used or overfished. Since the 1990s, overfishing of small **species** such as anchovies has affected larger sea creatures that hunt them, such as seals and seabirds. But many nations are now setting limits, called **quotas**, on the amount of fish that can be caught.

In addition, seals, dolphins, and turtles can get trapped in fishing nets and drown. Fortunately, nets are being designed with openings that allow creatures such as dolphins to escape.

These Pacific tuna are on sale in a Japanese market. Overfishing is making this species rare.

Dolphins need to surface regularly to breathe. This one has drowned after getting caught in a fishing net.

Collapse of the Newfoundland cod industry

Cod were once plentiful in the seas around Newfoundland, in Canada. But starting in the 1950s, these waters were heavily fished by deep-sea boats from Europe and Asia.

In 1976 Canada banned fishing boats from other countries. But it continued to catch 250,000 tonnes (275,500 tons) of cod a year itself. Experts warned of the danger of overfishing. But they were ignored. In 1992 there were almost no cod left to fish in Newfoundland. Cod fishing stopped, causing the loss of 40,000 jobs. Cod have not recovered in the area.

WORD BANK
overfishing   when so many fish are taken that not enough are left to have young
quota   maximum number of fish that can be caught during a certain period

Biodiversity

Earth has great **biodiversity**. About 1.75 million **species** of plants and animals have been identified so far. Unfortunately, scientists think that about 50 species die out a day. That is two every hour.

Hunting and the pet trade

Habitat loss is a major cause of species dying out. Hunting is another cause. In Africa, wild animals are sometimes killed for meat. They are also targeted for their fur, tusks, and other body parts. These are traded to people in other countries.

Some species are captured for sale as pets. Many creatures die during transportation. Others die because their owners do not provide the right conditions.

Protecting rare species

Most countries now have laws to protect **endangered** (at risk) wildlife. But some people still catch and sell them.

These shelves in the country of Honduras are full of crocodile skins. These skins will be made into purses, belts, and shoes.

European wildlife trade

The European Union (EU) is a group of 27 countries in Europe. The EU **imports** (buys from other countries) more wildlife products than anywhere else. Wildlife items sold according to the law make billions of dollars. Many people also try to sell items that break laws. In 2003 to 2004, the EU seized 7,000 shipments that were against the law. This included crocodile skins, snakeskins, and live lizards and snakes.

When governments find wildlife products that are against the law, they sometimes destroy them.

WORD BANK

import   buy and bring in something from another country

Population and Resources

According to one study, the wealthiest countries of the world use 86 percent of Earth's **natural resources**. But these countries make up just 20 percent of the world's total **population**. Meanwhile, in poorer places, people get by with very little.

Wasteful world

In **developed countries**, homes are full of machines and gadgets such as refrigerators, televisions, and laptops. All this technology is made available by **fossil fuels** and other resources. People end up throwing away a lot of what they buy quite quickly. This includes huge amounts of packaging. This way of life helps supports business. But it also involves a lot of waste.

In the world's richest nations, people spend money on a huge range of products.

Developing world

In the last 20 years or so, **developing countries** such as China and India have quickly started to develop factories and businesses. As more nations do this, more resources and **energy** are used. This adds to problems such as air **pollution** and **climate change**.

Car factories are becoming more common in developing countries such as India.

Lithium mining in Bolivia

Poor countries have the right to make money from their own resources. But **multinational** companies (companies that operate in several countries) often get involved. They pay to develop businesses such as **mining**. Then they often take most of the earnings.

For example, huge supplies of a metal called lithium have been located in the country of Bolivia, in South America. Lithium is used to run some vehicles. Multinational corporations are trying to take control of mining operations in Bolivia. They want to gain this valuable material at a low price. It is unlikely that Bolivia—a very poor country—will be able to benefit from its own resources.

WORD BANK
multinational   operating in several countries

Rising populations

The world's **population** is currently rising by 75 million people each year. Most of this growth is taking place in **developing countries**. There are often few **natural resources** there, such as land that is good for growing crops. This causes widespread hardship.

Seeking better opportunities and jobs, many people in developing countries move to cities. But too many people challenge a city's ability to provide services such as waste disposal. Many people end up living in poor conditions, or they are homeless.

Food and hunger

Experts say the world's farmers are able to grow enough food to feed everyone. But at the moment, this is not happening. The richest 30 percent of the world's population eats 60 percent of the world's food. Meanwhile, 935 million people do not get enough to eat. Most of these people live in the world's poorest countries.

In developing countries such as Kenya, in Africa, many people in cities end up living in poor areas like this.

In the United States, roughly half of the population is overweight. Just 4 percent suffers from not having enough food.

Wasting food

In **developed countries**, many people buy more food than they need. In the United States, one-quarter of all food is wasted.

People in these countries eat a lot of meat. Raising **livestock** such as beef cattle uses many natural resources, such as land and water. Far fewer resources are needed to grow crops. If fewer people ate meat, more food could be grown for everyone.

CASE STUDY

Hamburgers or rain forests?

Hamburgers are a popular fast food in countries like the United States. Over 20 ingredients go into, or are served with, every hamburger. Some of these products are bought from developing countries. In the United States, a lot of the beef used in hamburgers comes from cattle raised on ranches in the country of Brazil, in South America. Rain forests are cut down to clear land for raising cattle.

The global economy

Many products in our stores come from **developing countries**, such as India and China. However, transporting goods across the world by airplane, boat, and truck uses huge amounts of **fossil fuels**. This creates air **pollution**.

When multinational companies set the prices, local growers earn very little.

Imports and exports

Much of the food we buy in supermarkets also comes from developing countries in places like Africa. The governments of food-producing countries need the money from **exporting** these crops. But the trade is usually controlled by large **multinational** companies. They give farmers a low price for their food. In addition, the multinational companies often get to use the best land for themselves.

Flying fruits and vegetables from warm areas gives shoppers a wide choice. But it is a huge waste of **fuel**.

Fair trade

The fair trade movement gives farmers in developing countries a better deal. **Developed countries** establish trading partnerships with developing countries. The goal is to achieve fair prices and good working conditions for farmers in poorer parts of the world. For their part, growers must produce high-quality food. They must also not damage the **environment**. Fair trade products are usually a little more expensive. But the extra money is passed on to farmers in developing countries.

Find out more

When you visit a supermarket, read the labels on fruits and vegetables to find out the country they came from. Use a map to figure out how far the goods have traveled. Which product has traveled the farthest? Look for fair trade labels on products, too.

CASE STUDY

Two-way traffic

Scientists studying the movement of **imports** and exports have discovered something. International trade quite often involves a pointless, two-way traffic of almost identical goods. For example, in 2006 the United Kingdom exported 21 tonnes (23 tons) of bottled **mineral** water to Australia. It also imported 20 tonnes (22 tons) of Australian mineral water. What a waste!

Sustainable Living

By 2050 the world **population** will have grown by another two to three billion people. How can Earth provide the **natural resources** to support this number of people?

This can happen only if we change our habits. Otherwise, we will do lasting damage to the planet. We will also experience extreme shortages of food, water, wood, **fuel**, and more. Many people know they need to live more **sustainably**. But how can it be done?

Earth summits

In 1992 the world's countries met at the Earth Summit (meeting) in Rio de Janeiro, Brazil. Wealthy and poor nations agreed on a strategy for **sustainable development**. This breakthrough included a plan to deal with **global warming**. It also included a plan to save the natural world.

A Japanese leader gives a speech at the Millennium Development Goals Summit in 2010.

In 2000 **sustainability** was a main issue at the United Nations Millennium Summit. At this meeting, 192 world leaders agreed to maintain **biodiversity**. They also agreed to improve education and health in **developing countries**.

The way forward

Since then, governments worldwide have introduced plans to cut waste and **pollution**. For example, cities have introduced new, low-pollution kinds of public transportation. They offer benefits to companies that make changes to help the **environment**.

But we cannot leave it all to governments. It is up to each one of us to live less wastefully.

Bike-rental systems are encouraging people to use bicycles, rather than cars or buses, for short journeys around cities. The program shown here is in Taipei, Taiwan.

Find out more

The United Nations **Environment** Program recommends that 10 percent of each country's land should be set aside and protected from development. Find out how your country measures up by looking at http://mdgs.un.org/unsd/mdg/Data.aspx.

Conservation

Conservation is action taken to protect the natural world and wildlife. It protects important **natural resources**, such as forests. It protects wildlife by creating areas called wildlife **reserves** and national parks. There are now over 110,000 of these protected areas worldwide. They cover 12 percent of Earth's land.

Sustainable parks

Reserves need to be managed carefully. Their resources must be protected and **conserved** (protected for future use). **Mining** and development are limited or against the law.

Tourists can bring problems such as overcrowding, litter, and wearing away paths. Reserves and parks must find ways to manage these problems (see box on page 37).

The Northeast Greenland National Park, in Greenland, is the world's largest reserve. It covers 972,000 square kilometers (375,300 square miles).

A park worker describes wildlife in Saguaro National Park, in the state of Arizona. People at reserves work to educate the public about nature.

Sustainable forestry

Forests can be managed **sustainably**. People can select certain trees for cutting. It is also important to plant new trees. Products such as rubber can be gained without cutting down trees.

CASE STUDY

Park management in Yosemite National Park

Yosemite National Park, located in the state of California, is one of the most popular national parks in the United States. It is known for its beautiful cliffs, waterfalls, and Giant Sequoia trees.

Services for tourists such as campsites, restaurants, and bus services are all located together in a small area. This leaves almost 95 percent of the park as open wilderness. Hundreds of **species** of plants and animals are able to live safely. This plan also reduces the spread of negative effects of tourism, such as litter and traffic. Find out more about Yosemite at www.yosemite.national-park.com.

Preserving our resources

As we have seen, modern farming practices are damaging our **natural resources**. But **sustainable** farming practices allow farmers to protect the health of the soil, water, and more.

Organic farming does not use unnatural substances. Instead, organic farmers use natural **fertilizers** such as manure (animal waste). Pests may be controlled in natural ways. For example, farmers introduce ladybugs, which eat the pests. The practice of crop rotation (growing different crops each year) keeps the soil healthy.

Planting crops with deep roots and hedges restores land that is being worn away. These plants hold the land in place. Steep hillsides can be cut into steps. This protects soil and water.

Water conservation

A lack of water is threatening farming in many areas, from Africa to Australia. In the next few decades, **climate change** is likely to make these problems worse. Farmers can **conserve** water. They can use new **irrigation** techniques rather than wasteful water systems. A technique called **desalination** can be used to change seawater to freshwater. But this is very expensive.

The practice of growing several crops in one field helps to keep the soil healthy.

Water conservation in Israel

Israel is a dry country. New ideas in farming are helping farmers to conserve water. In a technique called drip irrigation, a group of pipes delivers moisture directly to crop roots.

Sometimes too much irrigation causes a buildup of natural salts in the soil. This problem can also be a problem in dry countries. Farmers are overcoming this by developing salt-resistant kinds of grapes and tomatoes. They are also avoiding crops, such as rice, that require a lot of water.

This drip irrigation system is being used to water young plants.

WORD BANK
desalination   technique that changes seawater to freshwater
organic   method of farming that only uses natural substances

Sustainable solutions

Sustainability is a huge challenge. We all need to make changes in our lives to preserve Earth's **natural resources**.

Saving energy and water at home

The **energy** we use at home is mostly created by using harmful **fossil fuels**. But we do not need to use as much energy. We can switch off lights and machines when we are not using them. And we can take a shower instead of a bath. This reduces the energy used to heat water. It also uses less water.

Reducing pollution

The simplest way to reduce **pollution** is to use cars less and public transportation more. Buying local foods prevents the pollution created by transporting goods. Look for **organic** foods. Or, better still, grow your own fruits and vegetables!

Recycling materials such as glass saves energy and natural resources.

Tackling waste

People can follow the "three Rs" of waste disposal—reduce, reuse, and **recycle**. (Recycling means reusing garbage so it can be made into other products.) Following the "three Rs" cuts pollution and energy use. Do not buy goods with too much packaging. Reuse plastic bags and containers. Recycle bottles, cans, paper, cardboard, and plastic. Simple steps like these can help to sustain our valuable resources.

CASE STUDY

Sustainable cities

Over half the world's **population** now lives in or near cities. By 2050 this will likely be true of two-thirds of the population. Rapidly growing cities draw heavily on local resources. They also suffer from pollution.

Many cities worldwide are now putting in place **sustainable** solutions. These solutions clean up the **environment** and improve living conditions. For example, many local governments are using non-polluting transportation. Land is being reused to become parks. Buildings are using the Sun's power to run lights and gadgets.

The panels on this roof in Paris, France, use the Sun's power. This provides sustainable energy.

Facts and Figures

Ecological footprints

This table shows the top-ten nations with the highest **ecological footprint** per person. This is measured as the amount of land needed to provide resources for one person.

Ranking	Country	Hectares (acres) needed to provide resources per person
1.	United Arab Emirates	15.99 (39.51)
2.	United States	12.22 (30.20)
3.	Kuwait	10.31 (25.48)
4.	Denmark	9.88 (24.41)
5.	New Zealand	9.54 (23.57)
6.	Ireland	9.43 (23.30)
7.	Australia	8.49 (20.98)
8.	Finland	8.45 (20.88)
9.	Canada	7.66 (18.93)
10.	Sweden	7.53 (18.61)

Source: www.nationmaster.com/graph/env_eco_foo-environment-ecological-footprint

Fishing

This shows the top-five countries with the largest fish catch in a year.

Ranking	Country	Size of catch in tonnes (tons)
1.	China	10,433,170 (11,500,600)
2.	Peru	7,490,730 (8,257,120)
3.	Chile	4,433,240 (4,886,810)
4.	Japan	3,593,660 (3,961,330)
5.	Russia	3,145,380 (3,467,190)

Source: www.nationmaster.com/graph/env_mar_fis_cat-environment-marine-fish-catch

Developed land

This shows the top-five countries with the greatest amount of developed land (land that has been cleared to become towns, factories, and more).

Ranking	Country	Percentage of total land area that is developed
1.	Belgium	43.93
2.	Netherlands	43.79
3.	Denmark	39.45
4.	Germany	32.84
5.	United Kingdom	32.05

Source: www.nationmaster.com/graph/env_non_wil-environment-non-wildness

Wilderness

This shows the top-five countries with the highest percentage of wilderness.

Ranking	Country	Percentage of wilderness
1.	Libya	89.90
2.	Canada	81.87
3.	Algeria	80.82
4.	Iceland	80.08
5.	Mauritania	79.46

Source: www.nationmaster.com/graph/env_wil-environment-wildness

Glossary

aquifer layer of rock or earth underground that holds water

atmosphere layer of gases that surrounds Earth

biodiversity variety of life in a particular area

biofuel fuel made by the stored energy of some plants

carbon dioxide colorless gas in the atmosphere

climate change change in the regular weather patterns of a region

conservation protecting the natural world

conserve protect or save for the future

deforestation clearing forestland of trees

desalination technique that changes seawater to freshwater

developed country wealthy country where many people live comfortably

developing country country where many people do not live comfortably

ecological footprint measure of human demands on Earth's resources. This term is sometimes also called a "global footprint."

endanger put at risk of dying out

energy ability to do work

environment natural world surrounding us on Earth

erosion when rock or soil is worn away by the action of wind, running water, or ice

evolve change over time to suit surroundings

export sell and transport something to another country

fertilizer substance that farmers use to make plants grow better

fossil fuel fuel, such as coal, oil, and natural gas, made of the remains of plants or animals that lived millions of years ago

fuel substance that can be used to create energy

gas substance without a definite shape, like air

global warming rising temperatures worldwide. This is caused by an increase of gases in the atmosphere that trap the Sun's heat.

graze feed on growing plants such as grass

greenhouse effect warming effect caused by certain gases in the air

habitat particular place that supports certain types of wildlife

import buy and bring in products from another country

irrigation method of controlling the flow of water through channels and other devices

livestock animals raised by farmers to provide food

mineral hard, natural substance. Minerals help provide everything from cement to gold.

mining removing valuable materials from the ground or deep below the surface

multinational operating in several countries

natural gas fuel gas found naturally in the ground

natural resource useful material found in nature, such as water or oil

nonrenewable describes resources, such as coal or oil, that will get used up

nuclear energy energy made by using uranium

ore mineral that contains a useful metal, such as copper

organic method of farming that does not use unnatural substances

overfishing when so many fish are taken that not enough are left to have young

pesticide substance that farmers use to control pests and weeds

pollution when the natural world is harmed by waste or by any substance that does not belong there

population number of people in an area

prairie largely treeless area of grassland

quota maximum number of fish that can be caught during a certain period

ray line or beam of energy

recycle reuse something so it can be turned into a new product

renewable describes a resource, such as the wind, that will not get used up

reserve area of land that is protected and carefully managed

sanitation removal of wastewater

species specific group of living things

sustainability using Earth's resources in a planned and careful way

sustainable when resources are managed so that they will not run out in the future, causing little damage to the environment

sustainable development managing economic growth and the way we live, without destroying resources that will be needed for the future

tailings waste rock left over from mining

Find Out More

Books

Belmont, Helen. *Planning for a Sustainable Future* (*Geography Skills*). Mankato, Minn.: Smart Apple Media, 2008.

Calhoun, Yael, ed. *Conservation* (*Environmental Issues*). Philadelphia: Chelsea House, 2005.

Gorman, Jacqueline Laks. *Fossil Fuels* (*What If We Do Nothing?*). Pleasantville, N.Y.: Gareth Stevens, 2009.

Green, Jen. *Reducing Air Pollution* (*Improving Our Environment*). Milwaukee: Gareth Stevens, 2005.

Green, Jen. *Saving Water* (*Improving Our Environment*). Milwaukee: Gareth Stevens, 2005.

Jakab, Cheryl. *Sustainable Cities* (*Global Issues*). Mankato, Minn.: Smart Apple Media, 2010.

Rooney, Anne. *Sustainable Water Resources* (*How Can We Save Our World?*). Mankato, Minn.: Arcturus, 2010.

Senker, Cath. *Sustainable Transportation* (*How Can We Save Our World?*). Mankato, Minn.: Arcturus, 2010.

Simon, Seymour. *Global Warming*. New York: Harper Collins, 2010.

Solway, Andrew. *Environmental Technology* (*New Technology*). Mankato, Minn.: Smart Apple Media, 2009.

Spilsbury, Richard. *The Great Outdoors: Saving Habitats* (*You Can Save the Planet*). Chicago: Heinemann Library, 2005.

Websites

www.footprintnetwork.org/en/index.php/GFN/page/earth_overshoot_day/
Learn more about ecological footprints at this Global Footprint Network website.

http://ase.org/programs/green-schools-program
Learn how the Alliance to Save Energy is trying to make schools more environmentally friendly with its "Green Schools" program.

www.epa.gov/kids/air.htm
This website of the U.S. Environmental Protection Agency provides facts about air pollution, including links that discuss climate change.

www.eere.energy.gov/kids/
This website, created by the U.S. Department of Energy Efficiency and Renewable Energy, offers games, tips, and facts to help young people save energy.

www.unfpa.org/public/
Learn more about what the United Nations Population Fund is doing to help improve the lives of people around the world.

www.wateraidamerica.org
Learn more about ways people are trying to get clean water to all parts of the world at this Water Aid website.

www.nps.gov/index.htm
Learn more about nature reserves at this website of the U.S. National Park Service.

www.greenpeace.org/usa/
Learn more about what the environmental group Greenpeace is doing to protect the environment.

www.foe.org
Learn more about how the environmental group Friends of the Earth is trying to save the environment.

www.worldwildlife.org /home-full.html
Learn more about the efforts of the World Wide Fund (WWF).

Index

air pollution 12, 29, 32, 35, 40
American Prairie Foundation 21
animals 5, 16, 18, 19, 20, 21,
    22, 24, 26, 31, 37
aquifers 16
Aral Sea 17
atmosphere 14, 15

biodiversity 20, 22, 26, 34, 35, 36
Bolivia 29

carbon dioxide 14, 15, 22
China 8, 28, 29, 32
cities 20, 30, 35, 41
climate change 15, 29, 34, 38
coal 4, 6, 10, 12, 14
cod fishing 25
conservation 36, 37, 38, 39, 40,
    41
copper mining 10, 11
crops 11, 19, 21, 30, 31, 32, 38,
    39

deep-level mining 10, 12
deforestation 5, 18, 22, 23, 31
desalination 38
desertification 18, 19
developing countries 8, 26, 28,
    29, 30, 31, 32, 33, 35
drinking water 16, 17

ecological footprint 8, 42
endangered species 20, 22, 26
energy 12, 13, 15, 23, 28, 29,
    32, 40, 41
environmentalism 6, 8, 22, 23, 26
erosion 18, 38, 39
European Union (EU) 27
exports 23, 26, 32, 33

fair trade movement 33
farming 5, 11, 14, 16, 17, 18, 19,
    20, 21, 22, 30, 32, 33, 38, 39
fertilizers 18, 38
fish 17, 18, 21, 24, 25, 42
food 5, 8, 16, 18, 20, 22, 30, 31,
    32, 33, 34, 40, 41
forests 4, 5, 6, 14, 18, 22, 23,
    31, 36, 37
fossil fuels 15, 28, 32, 40. See
    also coal; natural gas; oil.
freshwater 16, 17, 18, 38

global warming 14, 15, 22, 23, 34
governments 11, 12, 15, 20, 23,
    32, 35, 36, 41
grasslands 18, 20, 21
Great Plains 21
greenhouse effect 14, 15

habitats 20, 21, 22
housing 4, 12, 13, 20, 23, 28,
    30, 40, 41

imports 23, 26, 27, 32, 33
India 28, 29, 32
industries 12, 14, 16, 17, 18, 23,
    24, 25, 27, 28
insects 18, 38
international trade 23, 26, 27, 32,
    33
irrigation 17, 38, 39
Israel 39

lithium mining 29
livestock 18, 19, 31

Marcopper Mining Corporation 11
Millennium Summit 35
mining 10–11, 20, 23, 29, 36
multinational companies 29, 32

national parks 36, 37
natural gas 4, 12,
Newfoundland, Canada 25
nonrenewable resources 4, 10,
    12

oil 4, 6, 10, 12, 14, 41.
organic farming 38, 40
overfishing 24, 25

plants 5, 10, 18, 19, 20, 21, 22,
    26, 31, 37, 38, 39
pollution 4, 5, 10, 11, 12, 14, 17
    18, 20, 29, 32, 35, 40, 41
population 6, 17, 18, 20, 21, 28,
    30, 34, 41

renewable resources 5, 13, 15,
    22

Sahara Desert 19
soil 5, 10, 11, 14, 18, 19, 38, 39
surface mining 10
sustainability 6, 7, 22, 24, 34–35
    36, 37, 38, 40, 41

transportation 10, 12, 26, 32, 35
    40, 41
tropical rain forests 4, 22, 23, 31

United Kingdom 33
United Nations 17, 28, 30, 35,
    36, 41
United States 8, 16, 21, 28, 31,
    36, 37
uranium 11, 12

water 14, 15, 16, 17, 18, 21, 31
    33, 34, 38, 39, 40, 41
weather patterns 12, 15
wildlife trade 26, 27

Yosemite National Park 37